My Beloved Dog

PLACE YOUR PET'S I.D. INFORMATION OR PHOTO HERE.

MY DOG'S . . .

CALL NAME _____

BIRTHDAY _____

MICROCHIP # _____

OWNER(S) _____

_____

PHONE _____

_____

My Girl's Pet Record Book and Puppy Training Guide

The Ultimate Pet Health and Wellness Log, with Easy Tips to Raise and Train your Dog!

© 2020 Leila Grandemange   ISBN 978-0-9975658-5-0

ALL RIGHTS RESERVED: No part of this book may be reproduced, stored in a retrieval system, or transmitted in any form or by any means without the prior written permission of the publisher.

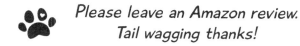
Please leave an Amazon review.
Tail wagging thanks!

DISCLAIMER: THE AUTHOR IS NOT A VET. The publisher and author are not responsible nor liable for any veterinary medical advice, course of treatment, diagnosis, or any other information obtained from this book. Please consult your veterinarian with questions about interpreting any information in this book.

References and resources provided are for informational purposes only. They do not necessarily represent the views of the author or publisher.

My Girl's

PET RECORD BOOK
AND PUPPY TRAINING GUIDE

The Ultimate Pet Health and Wellness Log, with Easy Tips to Raise and Train Your Dog!

By LEILA GRANDEMANGE

LEILAGRANDEMANGE.COM

Table of Contents

ABOUT THE BOOK 6

PART 1: OWNER AND DOG INFORMATION

Dog Owner Information 8
My Dog's Information 9
My Dog's Caregivers 10
Food, Medicine, Supplements 11
Trainers and Training Facilities 12
My Dog's Achievements... 13

PART 2: HEALTH CHARTS/MEDICAL HISTORY

Vaccination Log 16
Deworming Chart 18
Fecal Test Chart 19
Heartworm Screening & Prevention 20
Flea & Tick Control Log 21
Medications Record 22
Surgeries and Hospital Stays 24

PART 3: VET VISIT LOG/WELLNESS EXAMS

My Dog's Wellness Exams (space for 30 Checkups) 27

PART 4: PUPPY TRAINING & WELLNESS TIPS

Pet Parenting 101 60
10 Potty Training Tips 64
7 Crate Training Tips 66
6 Basic Training Tips 68
Socializing Your Puppy, Q & A 70

Dog Grooming Basics 72
16 Pet Safety Tips 75
Recognizing Signs of Sickness 78
Parasite Control Tips 80
Pet Insurance Guide 82

PART 5: RESOURCES & PRINTABLE FORMS

New Puppy Checklist 86
Puppy-Proofing Checklist 87
Pet Travel Checklist & To-Do's 88
Pet Sitter Forms 90
Dog Grooming Log 92
First Aid Kit for Pets 93
Pet Disaster Evacuation Checklist... 94
5 Things to do if You've Lost or Found a Dog 95
Phone Numbers Every Dog Owner Needs 96
Websites Every Dog Owner Needs 98
Note Pages 100
A Promise to My Pet 105

About the Author 106

> Dogs have a way of finding the people
> who need them, and filling an emptiness
> we didn't ever know we had.
>
> — Thom Jones

About the Book

CONGRATULATIONS on your new puppy, and thank you for making this book part of your pet parenting journey!

Bringing home a puppy or adult dog is like setting off on an exciting adventure! It's also a considerable responsibility, like parenting a child—you'll look after your dog's nutrition, training, grooming, and health records. It can be a lot to think about. That's where this book can help. You'll find detailed charts to organize your pet data and valuable tips to set your puppy off on a wholesome, happy path. Follow the prompts and fill out the pages. Then, sit back and enjoy the journey ahead!

This book is divided into five parts:

Part 1: Owner and Dog Profile

Part 2: Health Charts with Medical History

Part 3: Vet Visit Log/Wellness Exams

Part 4: Puppy Training and Wellness Tips

Part 5: Resources and Printable Forms

Reminder: Bring this book to each veterinary visit and update your pet's health status over the years. When leaving town, share this book with your pet sitter. Most importantly, keep it handy for emergencies. Having all your pet's medical history in one place can help you stay focused when needed most.

Happiness is a warm puppy.

— Charles Schulz

PART 1
Owner and Dog information

Dogs are not our whole life,
but they make our lives whole.

— Roger Caras

Owner Information

OWNER _____

Phone _____

Address _____

E-mail _____

Co-Owner _____

Phone _____

EMERGENCY CONTACTS

✚ Primary Vet _____

✚ Emergency Vet _____

Medical Insurance Policy _____

Family Contact _____

Pet Sitter/Walker _____

Pet Friendly Neighbor _____

Local Shelter _____

Animal Shelter _____

Police _____

Rescue Group _____

Microchip Company _____

Pet Friendly Hotel _____

Important phone numbers every dog owner needs—page 96

Pet Poison Helpline at 855-764-7661

My Dog's Information

CALL NAME _____

Registered Name _____

Sex _____ Born on _____

Color/Markings _____

Microchip # (be sure to register the chip) _____

Breed _____

AKC # _____

Type of Registration ☐ Limited   ☐ Full

Other Registry # _____ DNA # _____

Neutered/Spayed ☐ Yes   ☐ No

Date of Surgery _____

MY DOG CAME FROM . . .

Breeder Name/Phone _____

Rescue/Shelter/other _____

Date Acquired _____

Sire _____

Dam _____

My Dog's Care Givers

PRIMARY VET NAME _____

Phone/Email _____

Address _____

EMERGENCY VET NAME _____

Phone/Email _____

Address _____

Veterinary Specialists _____

_____

_____

Pet Sitter (s) (Sitter instruction form p.90)_____

_____

_____

Pet Walker _____

_____

Groomer (Grooming log, p.92) _____

_____

Doggie Day Care _____

_____

Other_____

_____

Food, Medicine & Supplements

MY DOG'S FOOD

Food brand and type (i.e., canned/dry/moist; raw/cooked):

_____

_____

Feeding Instructions (amount, how often?) _____

_____

_____

_____

Favorite Treats _____

_____

MEDICINE AND SUPPLEMENTS

Regular Medications (Medications log, page 22)

_____

_____

_____

Supplements_____

_____

_____

Allergies _____

_____

My Dog's Trainers

PRIMARY TRAINING FACILITY _____

Name _____

Phone/Email _____

Address _____

OTHER TRAINING FACILITIES, OBEDIENCE, AGILITY, etc.

Name _____

Phone/Email _____

Address _____

Name _____

Phone/Email _____

Address _____

Name _____

Phone/Email _____

Address _____

Notes: _____

_____

_____

_____

My Dog's Achievements

Record your dog's achievements: puppy and adult training classes completed, certifications, titles, awards, tricks learnec, etc. Have fun!

Achievement:_____Date _____

Achievement:_____Date _____

Achievement:_____Date _____

Achievement:_____Date _____

Achievement:_____Date _____

Achievement:_____Date _____

Achievement:_____Date _____

Achievement:_____Date _____

Achievement:_____Date _____

Achievement:_____Date _____

Achievement:_____Date _____

Achievement:_____Date _____

Achievement:_____Date _____

Achievement:_____Date _____

Achievement:_____Date _____

Achievement:_____Date _____

Everyone thinks they have the best
dog. And none of them is wrong.

— W.R. Purche

PART 2

Health Charts with Medical History

Vaccination Log

Deworming Chart

Fecal Exam Chart

Heartworm Prevention

Flea and Tick Control

Medications Record

Surgeries & Hospital Stays

Vaccination Log

Fill out this chart at your vet when your dog gets its shots.

AGE								
DATE								
Distemper								
Parvovirus								
Adenovirus2								
Parainfluenza								
Rabies								
Other								

Reminder: Complete the entire puppy vaccination series because maternal antibodies can last 14-16 weeks making earlier vaccines ineffective.

Notes _____
_____

Vaccination Log

For up-to-date vaccine guidelines visit www.aaha.org.

AGE								
DATE								
Distemper								
Parvovirus								
Adenovirus2								
Parainfluenza								
Rabies								
Other								

Notes: Record observations or adverse reactions to vaccines and the date.

_____
_____

Deworming Chart

Record the date, name of the deworming product, and dosage given.
Deworm and test for parasites per your vet's recommendations.

DATE	PRODUCT	DOSAGE

Parasite control tips are found on page 80.

Fecal Test Chart

Doing an annual fecal test by taking a sample of your dog's feces to your vet helps determine if specific parasites are present.

Date	Results	Recommendations

Parasite control tips are found on page 80.

Heartworm Screening & Prevention

Record annual heartworm blood testing and monthly meds. Parasite control tips, page 80.

Year	Test Result	Jan	Feb	Mar	Apr	May	June	July	Aug	Sept	Oct	Nov	Dec

Name of product/dosage/any adverse reactions_____

_____

Flea and Tick Control Log

Record flea and tick products given to your dog. Parasite control tips, page 80.

YEAR	Jan	Feb	Mar	Apr	May	June	July	Aug	Sept	Oct	Nov	Dec

Name of product/dosage/any adverse reactions_____

_____

Medications Record

Record the medications your dog takes regularly and throughout its life. Include parasite prevention meds. This will be vital information for you and your vet as your dog progresses through treatment, or in an emergency.

NAME OF MEDICATION _____

Dosage/Frequency _____

Reason for Medication _____

Reactions if any _____

Date _____ Prescribed by _____

NAME OF MEDICATION _____

Dosage/Frequency _____

Reason for Medication _____

Reactions if any _____

Date _____ Prescribed by _____

NAME OF MEDICATION _____

Dosage/Frequency _____

Reason for Medication _____

Reactions if any _____

Date _____ Prescribed by _____

NAME OF MEDICATION _____

Dosage/Frequency _____

Reason for Medication _____

Reactions if any _____

Date _____ Prescribed by _____

NAME OF MEDICATION _____

Dosage/Frequency _____

Reason for Medication _____

Reactions if any _____

Date _____ Prescribed by _____

NAME OF MEDICATION _____

Dosage/Frequency _____

Reason for Medication _____

Reactions if any _____

Date _____ Prescribed by _____

NAME OF MEDICATION _____

Dosage/Frequency _____

Reason for Medication _____

Reactions if any _____

Date _____ Prescribed by _____

NAME OF MEDICATION _____

Dosage/Frequency _____

Reason for Medication _____

Reactions if any _____

Date _____ Prescribed by _____

NAME OF MEDICATION _____

Dosage/Frequency _____

Reason for Medication _____

Reactions if any _____

Date _____ Prescribed by _____

NAME OF MEDICATION _____

Dosage/Frequency _____

Reason for Medication _____

Reactions if any _____

Date _____ Prescribed by _____

Notes _____

_____

_____

Surgeries and Hospital Stays

Record your dog's procedures (i.e., dental cleanings, spay/neuter), injuries, or illness.

DATE	WEIGHT	PROCEDURE/INJURY/ILLNESS	RESULTS	VET NAME

Surgery, Hospital Stay Notes

Record pre or post-op veterinary instructions and recommendations.

_____
_____
_____
_____
_____
_____
_____
_____
_____
_____
_____
_____
_____
_____
_____
_____
_____
_____
_____
_____
_____
_____
_____
_____

Dogs leave paw prints on our hearts.
—Unknown

PART 3
Vet Visit Log, Wellness Exams

Bring this book with you to the vet. Your notes will help you make informed decisions as you care for your beloved canine companion through each stage of its life.

MY DOG'S WELLNESS EXAM

DATE	WEIGHT	VETERINARIAN

REASON FOR VISIT:

Annual Wellness ☐ Vaccines ☐ Dental Check ☐

Fecal Exam ☐ Heartworm Test ☐ Other _____ ☐

QUESTIONS FOR MY VET _____

_____

_____

PROCEDURES DONE, VET COMMENTS OR RECOMMENDATIONS

_____

_____

_____

_____

TEST RESULTS _____

_____

MEDICATIONS PRESCRIBED _____

_____

DUE NEXT ON _____ **COST OF VISIT** _____

NOTES _____

_____

MY DOG'S WELLNESS EXAM

DATE	WEIGHT	VETERINARIAN

REASON FOR VISIT:

- Annual Wellness ☐
- Vaccines ☐
- Dental Check ☐
- Fecal Exam ☐
- Heartworm Test ☐
- Other _____ ☐

QUESTIONS FOR MY VET _____
_____
_____

PROCEDURES DONE, VET COMMENTS OR RECOMMENDATIONS
_____
_____
_____
_____

TEST RESULTS _____
_____

MEDICATIONS PRESCRIBED _____
_____

DUE NEXT ON _____ **COST OF VISIT** _____

NOTES _____
_____

MY DOG'S WELLNESS EXAM

DATE	WEIGHT	VETERINARIAN

REASON FOR VISIT:

- Annual Wellness ☐
- Vaccines ☐
- Dental Check ☐
- Fecal Exam ☐
- Heartworm Test ☐
- Other _____ ☐

QUESTIONS FOR MY VET _____
_____
_____

PROCEDURES DONE, VET COMMENTS OR RECOMMENDATIONS
_____
_____
_____
_____

TEST RESULTS _____
_____

MEDICATIONS PRESCRIBED _____
_____

DUE NEXT ON _____ **COST OF VISIT** _____

NOTES _____
_____

MY DOG'S WELLNESS EXAM

DATE	WEIGHT	VETERINARIAN

REASON FOR VISIT:

Annual Wellness ☐   Vaccines ☐   Dental Check ☐

Fecal Exam ☐   Heartworm Test ☐   Other _____ ☐

QUESTIONS FOR MY VET _____

_____

_____

PROCEDURES DONE, VET COMMENTS OR RECOMMENDATIONS

_____

_____

_____

_____

TEST RESULTS _____

_____

MEDICATIONS PRESCRIBED _____

_____

DUE NEXT ON _____   **COST OF VISIT** _____

NOTES _____

_____

MY DOG'S WELLNESS EXAM

DATE	WEIGHT	VETERINARIAN

REASON FOR VISIT:

- Annual Wellness ☐
- Vaccines ☐
- Dental Check ☐
- Fecal Exam ☐
- Heartworm Test ☐
- Other _____ ☐

QUESTIONS FOR MY VET _____

_____

_____

PROCEDURES DONE, VET COMMENTS OR RECOMMENDATIONS

_____

_____

_____

_____

TEST RESULTS _____

_____

MEDICATIONS PRESCRIBED _____

_____

DUE NEXT ON _____ **COST OF VISIT** _____

NOTES _____

_____

MY DOG'S WELLNESS EXAM

DATE	WEIGHT	VETERINARIAN

REASON FOR VISIT:

- Annual Wellness ☐
- Vaccines ☐
- Dental Check ☐
- Fecal Exam ☐
- Heartworm Test ☐
- Other _____ ☐

QUESTIONS FOR MY VET _____
_____
_____

PROCEDURES DONE, VET COMMENTS OR RECOMMENDATIONS
_____
_____
_____
_____

TEST RESULTS _____
_____

MEDICATIONS PRESCRIBED _____
_____

DUE NEXT ON _____ **COST OF VISIT** _____

NOTES _____
_____

MY DOG'S WELLNESS EXAM

DATE	WEIGHT	VETERINARIAN

REASON FOR VISIT:

- Annual Wellness ☐
- Vaccines ☐
- Dental Check ☐
- Fecal Exam ☐
- Heartworm Test ☐
- Other _____ ☐

QUESTIONS FOR MY VET _____

_____

_____

PROCEDURES DONE, VET COMMENTS OR RECOMMENDATIONS

_____

_____

_____

_____

TEST RESULTS _____

_____

MEDICATIONS PRESCRIBED _____

_____

DUE NEXT ON _____ **COST OF VISIT** _____

NOTES _____

_____

MY DOG'S WELLNESS EXAM

DATE	WEIGHT	VETERINARIAN

REASON FOR VISIT:

- Annual Wellness ☐
- Vaccines ☐
- Denta Check ☐
- Fecal Exam ☐
- Heartworm Test ☐
- Other _____ ☐

QUESTIONS FOR MY VET _____
_____
_____

PROCEDURES DONE, VET COMMENTS OR RECOMMENDATIONS
_____
_____
_____
_____

TEST RESULTS _____
_____

MEDICATIONS PRESCRIBED _____
_____

DUE NEXT ON _____ **COST OF VISIT** _____

NOTES _____
_____

MY DOG'S WELLNESS EXAM

DATE	WEIGHT	VETERINARIAN

REASON FOR VISIT:

- [ ] Annual Wellness
- [ ] Vaccines
- [ ] Dental Check
- [ ] Fecal Exam
- [ ] Heartworm Test
- [ ] Other _____

QUESTIONS FOR MY VET _____

_____

_____

PROCEDURES DONE, VET COMMENTS OR RECOMMENDATIONS

_____

_____

_____

_____

TEST RESULTS _____

_____

MEDICATIONS PRESCRIBED _____

_____

DUE NEXT ON _____ **COST OF VISIT** _____

NOTES _____

_____

MY DOG'S WELLNESS EXAM

DATE	WEIGHT	VETERINARIAN

REASON FOR VISIT:

- Annual Wellness ☐
- Vaccines ☐
- Dental Check ☐
- Fecal Exam ☐
- Heartworm Test ☐
- Other _____ ☐

QUESTIONS FOR MY VET _____

_____

_____

PROCEDURES DONE, VET COMMENTS OR RECOMMENDATIONS

_____

_____

_____

_____

TEST RESULTS _____

_____

MEDICATIONS PRESCRIBED _____

_____

DUE NEXT ON _____ **COST OF VISIT** _____

NOTES _____

_____

MY DOG'S WELLNESS EXAM

DATE	WEIGHT	VETERINARIAN

REASON FOR VISIT:

Annual Wellness ☐　　Vaccines ☐　　Dental Check ☐

Fecal Exam ☐　　Heartworm Test ☐　　Other _____ ☐

QUESTIONS FOR MY VET _____

_____

_____

PROCEDURES DONE, VET COMMENTS OR RECOMMENDATIONS

_____

_____

_____

_____

TEST RESULTS _____

_____

MEDICATIONS PRESCRIBED _____

_____

DUE NEXT ON _____ **COST OF VISIT** _____

NOTES _____

_____

MY DOG'S WELLNESS EXAM

DATE	WEIGHT	VETERINARIAN

REASON FOR VISIT:

Annual Wellness ☐   Vaccines ☐   Dental Check ☐

Fecal Exam ☐   Heartworm Test ☐   Other _____ ☐

QUESTIONS FOR MY VET _____

_____

_____

PROCEDURES DONE, VET COMMENTS OR RECOMMENDATIONS

_____

_____

_____

_____

TEST RESULTS _____

_____

MEDICATIONS PRESCRIBED _____

_____

DUE NEXT ON _____ **COST OF VISIT** _____

NOTES _____

_____

MY DOG'S WELLNESS EXAM

DATE	WEIGHT	VETERINARIAN

REASON FOR VISIT:

- Annual Wellness ☐
- Vaccines ☐
- Dental Check ☐
- Fecal Exam ☐
- Heartworm Test ☐
- Other _____ ☐

QUESTIONS FOR MY VET _____

_____

_____

PROCEDURES DONE, VET COMMENTS OR RECOMMENDATIONS

_____

_____

_____

_____

TEST RESULTS _____

_____

MEDICATIONS PRESCRIBED _____

_____

DUE NEXT ON _____ **COST OF VISIT** _____

NOTES _____

_____

MY DOG'S WELLNESS EXAM

DATE	WEIGHT	VETERINARIAN

REASON FOR VISIT:

- Annual Wellness ☐
- Vaccines ☐
- Dental Check ☐
- Fecal Exam ☐
- Heartworm Test ☐
- Other _____ ☐

QUESTIONS FOR MY VET _____

_____

_____

PROCEDURES DONE, VET COMMENTS OR RECOMMENDATIONS

_____

_____

_____

_____

TEST RESULTS _____

_____

MEDICATIONS PRESCRIBED _____

_____

DUE NEXT ON _____ **COST OF VISIT** _____

NOTES _____

_____

MY DOG'S WELLNESS EXAM

DATE	WEIGHT	VETERINARIAN

REASON FOR VISIT:

Annual Wellness ☐   Vaccines ☐   Dental Check ☐

Fecal Exam ☐   Heartworm Test ☐   Other _____ ☐

QUESTIONS FOR MY VET _____

_____

_____

PROCEDURES DONE, VET COMMENTS OR RECOMMENDATIONS

_____

_____

_____

_____

TEST RESULTS _____

_____

MEDICATIONS PRESCRIBED _____

_____

DUE NEXT ON _____ **COST OF VISIT** _____

NOTES _____

_____

MY DOG'S WELLNESS EXAM

DATE	WEIGHT	VETERINARIAN

REASON FOR VISIT:

- Annual Wellness ☐
- Vaccines ☐
- Dental Check ☐
- Fecal Exam ☐
- Heartworm Test ☐
- Other _____ ☐

QUESTIONS FOR MY VET _____

_____

_____

PROCEDURES DONE, VET COMMENTS OR RECOMMENDATIONS

_____

_____

_____

_____

TEST RESULTS _____

_____

MEDICATIONS PRESCRIBED _____

_____

DUE NEXT ON _____ **COST OF VISIT** _____

NOTES _____

_____

MY DOG'S WELLNESS EXAM

DATE	WEIGHT	VETERINARIAN

REASON FOR VISIT:

Annual Wellness ☐   Vaccines ☐   Dental Check ☐

Fecal Exam ☐   Heartworm Test ☐   Other _____ ☐

QUESTIONS FOR MY VET _____

_____

_____

PROCEDURES DONE, VET COMMENTS OR RECOMMENDATIONS

_____

_____

_____

_____

TEST RESULTS _____

_____

MEDICATIONS PRESCRIBED _____

_____

DUE NEXT ON _____ **COST OF VISIT** _____

NOTES _____

_____

MY DOG'S WELLNESS EXAM

DATE	WEIGHT	VETERINARIAN

REASON FOR VISIT:

- Annual Wellness ☐
- Vaccines ☐
- Dental Check ☐
- Fecal Exam ☐
- Heartworm Test ☐
- Other _____ ☐

QUESTIONS FOR MY VET _____

_____

_____

PROCEDURES DONE, VET COMMENTS OR RECOMMENDATIONS

_____

_____

_____

_____

TEST RESULTS _____

_____

MEDICATIONS PRESCRIBED _____

_____

DUE NEXT ON _____ **COST OF VISIT** _____

NOTES _____

_____

MY DOG'S WELLNESS EXAM

DATE	WEIGHT	VETERINARIAN

REASON FOR VISIT:

Annual Wellness ☐   Vaccines ☐   Dental Check ☐

Fecal Exam ☐   Heartworm Test ☐   Other _____ ☐

QUESTIONS FOR MY VET _____

_____

_____

PROCEDURES DONE, VET COMMENTS OR RECOMMENDATIONS

_____

_____

_____

_____

TEST RESULTS _____

_____

MEDICATIONS PRESCRIBED _____

_____

DUE NEXT ON _____   **COST OF VISIT** _____

NOTES _____

_____

MY DOG'S WELLNESS EXAM

DATE	WEIGHT	VETERINARIAN

REASON FOR VISIT:

- Annual Wellness ☐
- Vaccines ☐
- Denta Check ☐
- Fecal Exam ☐
- Heartworm Test ☐
- Other _____ ☐

QUESTIONS FOR MY VET _____

_____

_____

PROCEDURES DONE, VET COMMENTS OR RECOMMENDATIONS

_____

_____

_____

_____

TEST RESULTS _____

_____

MEDICATIONS PRESCRIBED _____

_____

DUE NEXT ON _____ **COST OF VISIT** _____

NOTES _____

_____

MY DOG'S WELLNESS EXAM

DATE	WEIGHT	VETERINARIAN

REASON FOR VISIT:

- Annual Wellness ☐
- Vaccines ☐
- Dental Check ☐
- Fecal Exam ☐
- Heartworm Test ☐
- Other _____ ☐

QUESTIONS FOR MY VET _____

_____

_____

PROCEDURES DONE, VET COMMENTS OR RECOMMENDATIONS

_____

_____

_____

_____

TEST RESULTS _____

_____

MEDICATIONS PRESCRIBED _____

_____

DUE NEXT ON _____ **COST OF VISIT** _____

NOTES _____

_____

MY DOG'S WELLNESS EXAM

DATE	WEIGHT	VETERINARIAN

REASON FOR VISIT:

Annual Wellness ☐   Vaccines ☐   Dental Check ☐

Fecal Exam ☐   Heartworm Test ☐   Other _____ ☐

QUESTIONS FOR MY VET _____

_____

_____

PROCEDURES DONE, VET COMMENTS OR RECOMMENDATIONS

_____

_____

_____

_____

TEST RESULTS _____

_____

MEDICATIONS PRESCRIBED _____

_____

DUE NEXT ON _____ **COST OF VISIT** _____

NOTES _____

_____

MY DOG'S WELLNESS EXAM

DATE	WEIGHT	VETERINARIAN

REASON FOR VISIT:

Annual Wellness ☐   Vaccines ☐   Dental Check ☐

Fecal Exam ☐   Heartworm Test ☐   Other _____ ☐

QUESTIONS FOR MY VET _____

_____

_____

PROCEDURES DONE, VET COMMENTS OR RECOMMENDATIONS

_____

_____

_____

_____

TEST RESULTS _____

_____

MEDICATIONS PRESCRIBED _____

_____

DUE NEXT ON _____ **COST OF VISIT** _____

NOTES _____

_____

MY DOG'S WELLNESS EXAM

DATE	WEIGHT	VETERINARIAN

REASON FOR VISIT:

- Annual Wellness ☐
- Vaccines ☐
- Dental Check ☐
- Fecal Exam ☐
- Heartworm Test ☐
- Other _____ ☐

QUESTIONS FOR MY VET _____

_____

_____

PROCEDURES DONE, VET COMMENTS OR RECOMMENDATIONS

_____

_____

_____

_____

TEST RESULTS _____

_____

MEDICATIONS PRESCRIBED _____

_____

DUE NEXT ON _____ **COST OF VISIT** _____

NOTES _____

_____

MY DOG'S WELLNESS EXAM

DATE	WEIGHT	VETERINARIAN

REASON FOR VISIT:

Annual Wellness ☐   Vaccines ☐   Dental Check ☐
Fecal Exam ☐   Heartworm Test ☐   Other _____ ☐

QUESTIONS FOR MY VET _____

_____

_____

PROCEDURES DONE, VET COMMENTS OR RECOMMENDATIONS

_____

_____

_____

_____

TEST RESULTS _____

_____

MEDICATIONS PRESCRIBED _____

_____

DUE NEXT ON _____ **COST OF VISIT** _____

NOTES _____

_____

MY DOG'S WELLNESS EXAM

DATE	WEIGHT	VETERINARIAN

REASON FOR VISIT:

- Annual Wellness ☐
- Vaccines ☐
- Denta Check ☐
- Fecal Exam ☐
- Heartworm Test ☐
- Other _____ ☐

QUESTIONS FOR MY VET _____

_____

_____

PROCEDURES DONE, VET COMMENTS OR RECOMMENDATIONS

_____

_____

_____

_____

TEST RESULTS _____

_____

MEDICATIONS PRESCRIBED _____

_____

DUE NEXT ON _____ **COST OF VISIT** _____

NOTES _____

_____

MY DOG'S WELLNESS EXAM

DATE	WEIGHT	VETERINARIAN

REASON FOR VISIT:

Annual Wellness ☐   Vaccines ☐   Dental Check ☐

Fecal Exam ☐   Heartworm Test ☐   Other _____ ☐

QUESTIONS FOR MY VET _____

_____

_____

PROCEDURES DONE, VET COMMENTS OR RECOMMENDATIONS

_____

_____

_____

_____

TEST RESULTS _____

_____

MEDICATIONS PRESCRIBED _____

_____

DUE NEXT ON _____   **COST OF VISIT** _____

NOTES _____

_____

MY DOG'S WELLNESS EXAM

DATE	WEIGHT	VETERINARIAN

REASON FOR VISIT:

- [ ] Annual Wellness
- [ ] Vaccines
- [ ] Dental Check
- [ ] Fecal Exam
- [ ] Heartworm Test
- [ ] Other _____

QUESTIONS FOR MY VET _____

_____

_____

PROCEDURES DONE, VET COMMENTS OR RECOMMENDATIONS

_____

_____

_____

_____

TEST RESULTS _____

_____

MEDICATIONS PRESCRIBED _____

_____

DUE NEXT ON _____ **COST OF VISIT** _____

NOTES _____

_____

MY DOG'S WELLNESS EXAM

DATE	WEIGHT	VETERINARIAN

REASON FOR VISIT:

- Annual Wellness ☐
- Vaccines ☐
- Dental Check ☐
- Fecal Exam ☐
- Heartworm Test ☐
- Other _____ ☐

QUESTIONS FOR MY VET _____

_____

_____

PROCEDURES DONE, VET COMMENTS OR RECOMMENDATIONS

_____

_____

_____

_____

TEST RESULTS _____

_____

MEDICATIONS PRESCRIBED _____

_____

DUE NEXT ON _____ **COST OF VISIT** _____

NOTES _____

_____

MY DOG'S WELLNESS EXAM

DATE	WEIGHT	VETERINARIAN

REASON FOR VISIT:

- Annual Wellness ☐
- Vaccines ☐
- Dental Check ☐
- Fecal Exam ☐
- Heartworm Test ☐
- Other _____ ☐

QUESTIONS FOR MY VET _____

_____

_____

PROCEDURES DONE, VET COMMENTS OR RECOMMENDATIONS

_____

_____

_____

_____

TEST RESULTS _____

_____

MEDICATIONS PRESCRIBED _____

_____

DUE NEXT ON _____ **COST OF VISIT** _____

NOTES _____

_____

Properly trained, a man can be dog's best friend.

— Corey Ford

PART 4

Puppy Training and Wellness Tips

Pet Parenting 101

10 Potty Training Tips

7 Crate Training Tips

6 Basic Training Tips

Socializing your Puppy, Q & A

Dog Grooming Basics

16 Pet Safety Tips

Recognizing Signs of Sickness

Parasite Control Tips

Pet Insurance Guide

# Pet Parenting 101

RAISING A PUPPY is a wonderfully magical (and sometimes messy) journey! It is also a considerable responsibility, kind of like parenting a child. Below are 17 useful tips on how to keep your fur baby happy, healthy, and safe at each stage of its life. Don't hesitate to consult a vet with questions about your dog's well-being.

1. PUPPY PROOF YOU HOME: Your dog depends on you to keep it safe. So you'll want to puppy-proof your home before the arrival of your new puppy. Move anything toxic to a dog, "chewable," or breakable, out of reach. Ensure electric cords are inaccessible and block any part of the house you want off limits. Also, check the yard to be sure your dog is safe, secure, and contained (i.e., inspect for fenced areas vulnerable to chewing and digging out). For a puppy proofing checklist, see page 87. Also visit akc.org/expert-advice/ and type "Puppy Proofing Tips" in the search bar.

2. PREPARE YOUR PUPPY STUFF: Besides puppy-proofing, you're probably excited to prepare your "puppy stuff," such as purchasing your pet's I.D., a cute collar and leash, and fun toys! Check out the "New Puppy Checklist" on page 86 and pet shopping sites on page 99.

3. CHOOSE A VET ASAP: Within the first few days of arrival, you'll want to have your pup examined by a veterinarian. Your vet will verify your pup's general health, implant a microchip if needed, set up a vaccination schedule, create an individualized wellness plan, and address any concerns. Keep your vet's number (and emergency vet number) handy. Page 78—Recognizing Signs of a Sick Dog.

4. SCHEDULE CHECK-UPS: Taking your dog to the vet at least annually lets you verify their general health and track things like weight, dental health, and vaccines. Never hesitate to contact your vet if your dog appears ill or in pain. Record check-ups on pp. 28-57.

5. VACCINATE: Vaccinations are given to protect animals from diseases, many of which can affect people (i.e., rabies). Discuss with your vet the vaccine protocol that best considers your puppy's age, health, environment, and lifestyle to maintain appropriate immunity. Record vaccines on pages 16-17.

6. CONTROL PARASITES: Parasites of dogs can cause discomfort and health issues to your dog and can also infect family members. Thankfully, there are preventative measures you can take to protect everyone. See page 80 for parasite control tips.

7. FEED A HEALTHY DIET: Not all dog foods are equal. Choose a high-quality dog food best suited to your dog's size, age, and activity level. Keep feeding times regular, measure the food to prevent obesity, and always provide fresh, clean water. If you change foods, gradually introduce the new food over a 7-day period by mixing the new food with the old. Learn about the pros and cons of feeding dry and/or wet; raw and/or cooked; homemade or commercial food. Dogfoodadvisor.com provides useful pet food guidance.

8. EXERCISE YOUR DOG: Dogs need regular exercise to ensure their physical and mental health and to prevent obesity. Exercise should be appropriate to your dog's age and energy level. Take your dog for a daily walk, throw the ball in the yard, or engage your dog in any activity that will get them up and moving. You can also call your local dog club or training center to see what activities are offered.

9. GROOM REGULARLY: Dog grooming is not just about bathing and brushing your dog. It involves all aspects of canine hygiene and cleanliness, including things like cleaning ears, clipping nails, and tooth brushing. Regular grooming can be an enjoyable bonding time, as well as alert you to possible health issues— i.e., you may discover a tick or a lump. Refer to page 72 for grooming tips. A printable grooming log is on page 92.

10. POTTY TRAIN YOUR POOCH: Dogs need to relieve themselves regularly, and the younger the dog, the more often they will need to go potty. See page 64 for potty training basics.

11. CRATE TRAIN: Crates are used for various purposes such as sleep, travel safety, and potty training. See p. 66 for crate training tips.

12. MAKE HOUSE RULES: Get the whole family on board. Decide what is OK and NOT in the house (i.e., jumping on the sofa, sleeping in bed). Make sure everyone sticks to the rules. Consistency will help your dog grow into a well-behaved pet.

13. AVOID SEPARATION ANXIETY: Teaching your puppy early on to be alone for short periods can help avoid separation anxiety. When you leave the house, try playing soft music and offering your pet some sturdy, safe toys to keep them occupied. Leave and come home with minimum fuss so they will learn not to worry about your coming and going. Keep in mind that dogs cannot be expected to thrive if left alone for long hours regularly. Use a pet sitter, mid-day dog walker, or doggie daycare if needed.

14. TRAIN AND SOCIALIZE: Properly done, basic obedience training builds confidence and self-esteem and can protect your pet for life. A well-mannered dog also makes dog ownership much more enjoyable. Training goes hand in hand with *socialization*—the process of gently exposing a puppy to a wide variety of people, places, and situations it may encounter as an adult. Proper socialization positively shapes a puppy's future personality. See page 68 for basic training tips and page 70 for socialization tips.

15. PREPARE FOR PUBERTY: Puppy puberty (the "teen years,") involves behavioral and physical changes, and the ability to reproduce, so you'll want to take steps to prevent unwanted breeding. At some point, you may think about spaying or neutering. The decision if and when to spay or neuter depends on many factors, which your vet can advise you on. **Here are some tips to help you anticipate puberty and keep your fur babies safe:**

- **Watch for changes** to know when puberty is approaching. Most puppies usually hit "puberty" (the beginning of sexual maturity) around 6-9 months, but this can vary. Smaller dogs tend to come in earlier while larger breeds may wait until two years of age.

- **Male "teens"** get a testosterone boost at puberty, which can lead to behavior changes, such as mounting objects, people, and other dogs, "marking," or becoming tense around other male dogs. Thankfully, with training, you can curb most unwanted behavior. Tip: *Belly Bands* can be found online to help with marking issues.

- **Female puberty** is a bit more complex since you will also deal with her heat cycle. These are some signs she is coming in heat (also known as "in season"): Her vulva will swell. She will lick and clean the area, urinate more often, and develop a blood-tinged vaginal discharge for about 7-10 days. Be alert; she can be fertile for about 2-3 weeks. Also, she may feel a bit anxious during this delicate time, so avoiding unnecessary outings, training classes, and meeting new people is a good idea. Tip: *Period panties* for dogs can be found online. They are used to prevent her discharge from staining furniture and clothing.

- **Be extra vigilant** when she's in heat. Accompany her at all times (on leash), even in the yard, and keep her away from male dogs. And be sure she is out of heat before letting her around male dogs. Once out of season, a bath or visit to the groomers is nice. Note: A female dog comes in heat about every six months unless spayed.

- **Finally, as always, keep your dogs secure** and under careful watch. Your puppy may be fertile before you realize it. By being prepared, you won't be caught off guard.

16. USE PET-SAFE CLEANING PRODUCTS: Raising a puppy has its messy moments. Be sure your cleaning products are safe for pets. Dogs' paws touch the floor, and their noses are close too. Most commercial cleaning products contain potentially hazardous ingredients, such as bleach, ammonia, and perfumes, that can irritate a dog's eyes and skin and cause breathing problems.

Opt for pet-safe cleaning products with ingredients such as vinegar, baking soda, lemon juice, and hydrogen peroxide. To learn more, visit akc.org/expert-advice—search "5 Dog-Safe Cleaning Solutions You Can Mix at Home." Note: These cleaners should not be confused with disinfectants used to combat viruses like COVID-19. For that purpose, consult the *Environmental Protection Agency* (EPA). Keep your pet at a safe distance if you must use stronger cleaning products.

17. KNOW CHANGING NEEDS: As your dog progresses from puppyhood through old age, its specific needs will change. For example, an older dog may need more frequent potty breaks or a special diet. Take time to learn the best ways to care for your dog's emotional and physical well-being at each stage of its life.

I wish people would realize that animals
are totally dependent on us, helpless, like
children, a trust that is put upon us.

— James Herriot

10 Potty Training Tips

DOGS NEED TO relieve themselves often, and the younger the dog, the more often they need to go. By following these housetraining tips, your pup will be on its way to potty training success! Just remember, potty training a puppy takes time. So practice patience.

1. **KEEP CONSTANT WATCH** over your puppy. Young pups are still developing control of their bladders and need constant supervision until they are reliably housetrained. Don't expect a puppy to be fully potty trained until about 6-8 months old. Even then, be aware of its needs. Each dog is different.

2. **CONTAIN YOUR PUPPY** when you cannot supervise it. Using a crate is an excellent housetraining tool because dogs will generally not eliminate in their "home." Train your puppy to be happy in his cozy abode (see page 66). Try placing the crate near or in your bedroom. This way, you can hear if your pup whines to go out at night. Expand your dog's freedom in the house gradually.

3. **WATCH FOR SIGNS** your puppy needs to go potty—If you see your puppy pace, whine, circling and sniffing the floor, grab the leash and get out the door. Puppies will want to relieve themselves first thing in the morning, last thing at night, after they play, nap, spend time in a crate, chewing on a bone or toy, and drinking. While your dog is active, take it out at least once an hour and even more in the morning and evening.

4. **COMMIT TO A CONSISTENT SCHEDULE** for food, water, and walks while housetraining. Timing is everything! A daily potty training schedule may look like this:

- *Morning routine:* Take your pup out first thing. Then, feed breakfast (aim for the same time each day). Always provide fresh water. Allow your dog 15 minutes or so to eat, and remove the bowl. Then wait between 5-30 minutes and take it out again.

- *Meal times:* Most pups eat 3-4 meals a day. Take your puppy out right after each meal, also after drinking water.

- *After naps and playtime:* During the day, your pup may nap every hour or so. As soon as it wakes up, take it out to potty. Playtime can also give your pup the urge to potty. So keep a watchful eye for signs, as mentioned on page 64.
- *Before bedtime:* Remember to take your puppy out to potty one last time before you go to bed at night.

5. **CHOOSE A "POTTY SPOT"** and try to use the same door to the same area you'd like your dog to eliminate. Keep your puppy on a leash (even in a fenced yard), so you can react quickly with a reward. Stand quietly in the chosen "potty spot." When you see your pup commence, use a signal or voice command (i.e., "go potty"). Once finished, offer lavish praise and a yummy treat!

6. **TRY PLACING A BELL** on the door handle and train your pup to ring the bell to go out to potty. Ring it each time you take it out. Praise your dog when it rings it on its own.

7. **OFFER ENTHUSIASTIC PRAISE** ("good boy!") and reward your dog when it eliminates in the right place. Never hit or yell at your dog when it has an accident. Instead, if you catch your dog in the act inside the house, make a noise to get its attention (i.e., say "uh-oh," firmly yet gently) and immediately take it outside. Wait until it finishes, then offer praise and reward.

8. **TAKE TIME TO PLAY** together after your dog eliminates. If you bring your pup inside right after it goes potty, it will learn that play-time stops when it urinates.

9. **REMOVE ALL TRACES OF ODOR** if your puppy has an "accident" in the house, or your pup will continue to go to that spot to relieve itself. To remove urine and feces odors, enzymatic neutralizers, such as Nature's Miracle, are recommended rather than household detergents.

10. **PLAN AHEAD** when leaving your pup home. Use the *month-plus-one rule* (see P.67) to know the maximum time your puppy can comfortably hold its bladder until your return.

♡ 7 Crate Training Tips

CRATE TRAINING is giving your dog a comfy "den-like" space of its own to feel safe and secure. Never use a crate for punishment. Your dog should associate its crate with peaceful, happy things.

Follow these tips to help you crate train your puppy:

1. Introduce your pup to the crate gradually in small increments of time while you are home.

2. Line the crate with comfortable bedding or blankets and fill it with a few sturdy, safe toys. Make sure the crate is well ventilated and in a comfortable and relaxed environment.

3. Try tossing some treats to the back of the crate or offer a meal there. If your puppy goes in, gently close the door for a couple of minutes and then let it back out.

4. Increase the time in the crate by 5-10-minute increments daily until you get to an hour. Keep the crate near your activities. Take your puppy outside to eliminate immediately after taking it out of the crate.

5. Speak to your dog now and then while it's learning to be in a crate. Also, offer your pup a treat to let it know it's a good doggie for calmly lying there. Then, when it's time to leave your puppy alone, you'll have a happy, calm, crate-trained dog.

6. The time your puppy spends in a crate should be limited, with regular breaks for exercise, social contact, urination, and defecation. If left too long in a crate, your pup may be forced to relieve itself on the bedding. When a dog has an accident in the crate, it is not because it misbehaved. Instead, someone neglected the responsibility to take it out.

7. Use the *month-plus-one rule.* Pups cannot hold their bladder as long as an adult. If you're unsure how long your puppy can hold its bladder comfortably while in a crate (for example when you leave home to run an errand), the American Kennel club recommends using the "month-plus-one" rule:

The Month-plus-one rule

"Take the age of your puppy in months and add one, and that is the maximum number of hours that your pup should be able to comfortably hold it between potty breaks A 3-month-old puppy plus one equals 4 hours that they should be able to stay in the crate without a mess" (Harriet Meyers, AKC.org).

More useful tips:

- Crates come in various sizes, materials, and shapes and can be used for multiple containment purposes, such as for sleep, travel, potty training, or in case of emergency. Depending on your intended use, you may need one or more crates. For example, many dog owners choose a smaller sturdy crate for car travel, and a larger wire crate for home use.

- When used as a housetraining tool, the size of the crate should be just large enough for the dog to stand up tall, turn around, fully stretch out and lie down comfortably. The limited space teaches your pup to "hold it" because dogs will naturally avoid stepping on their waste. Some larger crates come with dividers to help you achieve this goal while your puppy is still young.

- Use the crate for "quiet-time" when needed—i.e., suppose you're having a party or there are workers in the home. In that case, your puppy will appreciate a calm space to feel secure.

- Use the crate for puppy "nap-time." Your puppy will find it easier to unwind away from the family commotion.

- Limited crate time is essential for seniors and dogs with special health concerns. Elderly dogs may have trouble holding their bladder and may need to go out more often.

6 Basic Training Tips

1. PRAISE OFTEN

The sweetest sound to a dog's ear is the sound of praise! Our happy, enthusiastic tone when we say "Yes!" or "Good girl!" lets our dogs know they've understood what was asked of them. The tone of our voice, yummy treats, toys, and play are all forms of praise and reward. Praise your dog lavishly when it obeys you, and use positive training methods. If a dog doesn't do what you've asked, do not assume it is being disobedient. As dog owners, we must learn how to read our dog's body language and adjust our behavior to communicate better what we expect. That is why training classes often benefit the owner as much, if not more, than the dog.

2. OFFER LOVING LEADERSHIP

Every dog needs a human who can lead them. But leadership is often misunderstood. It does not mean we use force or intimidation to dominate our dog. Instead, we lead more like a partner in a dance. If you're unsure how to do that, a professional dog trainer can help. There are also many good books and online articles on the topic. Take time to understand how dogs communicate and how to train them using kind and loving directions. This way, you can avoid training mishaps and help your pup grow into a well-trained, happy dog that's a joy to live with!

3. TEACH BASIC COMMANDS

Whether you enroll in formal training or not, every dog needs to learn basic commands—*Come, Heel, Sit, Stay, and Down.* Discuss with your vet the best timing (based on your pup's vaccine schedule) to enroll in puppy kindergarten. Go loaded with praise and treats, and enjoy your puppy. Consider going further by enrolling in more advanced obedience classes.

 To learn more: download your free akc ebook at www.akc.org called "The Five Commands Every Dog Should Know."

4. KEEP THINGS SHORT AND SWEET

Puppies have short attention spans and can burn out if trained for too long. Set your pup up for success by keeping sessions 1-2 minutes. Try mini-training sessions throughout your day. Keep it fun and set reasonable expectations for each session. Always end on a positive note with praise, treats, or playtime.

5. PLAY WITH YOUR POOCH

Playing with your dog is a great way to teach it to obey. It is also one of the best ways to keep your pet happy and healthy, and it's good for owners too! Playing with your pooch should always be a positive experience. Try games such as fetch, hide-and-seek, find-the-treat, tug of war, swimming, Frisbee, and soccer, and discover what you and your dog enjoy.

These are a few of the benefits of playing with your dog:

- Using play, combined with rewards and treats, is a great way to encourage good behavior.
- Prevents boredom and destructive behavior by providing the opportunity for mental and physical stimulation. Dogs love having the chance to use their instinctive behaviors such as running, jumping, sniffing, and searching for things.
- Strengthens the bond between you and your pet, encourages communication, and creates loyalty.
- Running, chasing, jumping, and swimming can help keep your dog fit, build muscle, and prevent obesity and diabetes.

6. PARTICIPATE IN ACTIVITIES WITH YOUR DOG

Numerous organizations, such as the American Kennel Club, offer activities and sports for dogs. Here are a few: Obedience, Agility, Conformation, Rally, Freestyle, Tracking, Field Events, and Pet Therapy. Also, check with your local dog clubs and training centers for a list of activities, meet-ups, and classes. Of course, there are also simple pleasures to enjoy with your dog, such as taking a walk in the park, jogging, or playing in the yard.

Puppy Socialization Q & A

WHAT IS SOCIALIZATION?

Socialization is the ongoing process in which a puppy is gently introduced to things they may encounter as an adult, such as new people, animals, stimuli, and environments. The first 3-4 months of life are the prime window of opportunity for pups to experience new things because it's the period when sociability outweighs fear. Proper socialization is key to helping your puppy grow into a happy, well-adjusted adult. Below is a brief overview of the process.

WHEN DO I BEGIN?

Most reputable breeders will have already begun the socialization process. You can continue that process in the safety of your home as soon as you pick up your puppy. Then, once your vet says it's safe, you can start taking your dog out to public places, so it can meet new people and learn how to behave in various situations.

HOW DO I SOCIALIZE MY PUPPY?

- **Take baby steps.** Gradually introduce your puppy to spaces in your home where it feels secure. Encourage your puppy to explore at its own pace while under your watchful eye. As it gets older (with your vet's approval), you can venture out to more places, starting small. Gently expose your puppy to things that move it out of its comfort zone and build confidence.

- **Handle your puppy gently early on,** so it will learn to accept being touched on all parts of its body. Involve the family, keeping a careful watch when small children handle puppies.

- **Gradually expose your puppy to new** and different things—such as new sights, sounds, smells, people, well-socialized animals, and various places. Begin at home with interactive toys, games, steps, and tunnels. Also, place your puppy on various surfaces to enrich its environment and take it on as many car trips as possible. As your puppy grows, it can visit other homes to get used to more people and stimuli. Eventually, it will graduate to quiet public places, followed by more busy areas.

- **Enroll in puppy class.** Once your pup has started vaccinations, it can also attend puppy classes. But it's always wise to check with your vet first. These classes, led by skilled trainers, are designed to teach basic commands and expose your puppy to other canines and people. You can find puppy classes through dog training facilities and local AKC training clubs.

- **Keep socialization fun**. Use positive reinforcement with frequent praise and rewards—petting, play, and/or treats.
- **Plan a puppy play date.** Inviting friends with vaccinated, well-mannered dogs can be a fun way to introduce your puppy to other dogs in a relaxed yet controlled setting. Keep puppy parties small, short, and sweet to begin (about a half hour). Later, you can increase it to 1 hour and enlarge your parties to include small children and more adults. Ask guests to give your puppy bits of its favorite treat to help your dog associate being around people with a fun and rewarding time.

 For a comprehensive puppy socialization checklist, visit leemakennels.com/blog/puppies/puppy-socialisation-checklist/.

WHAT ABOUT OLDER DOGS?

Even though an older dog has passed the prime window of socialization, there's still lots you can do, especially with the help of an experienced trainer. Help your dog associate new or fearful situations with positive experiences. Slowly reintroduce your dog to new sights, smells, and sounds, always under careful supervision and with lots of praise and treats. Severe behavioral problems (i.e., fearfulness) should be treated with the help of a veterinarian and/or animal behaviorist.

Important: Until completion of the full puppy vaccination series (7-10 days after the last vaccine), limit your puppy's exposure to well-vaccinated healthy dogs, always being careful where your puppy is walked. Avoid dog parks and areas that are not sanitized and/or highly trafficked by dogs of unknown vaccination or disease status. Tip: Suggest a vet do an antibody titer to access vaccine-induced immunity.

Puppy Play Date!

Dog Grooming Basics

A printable dog grooming log is found on page 92.

DOG GROOMING involves all aspects of canine hygiene, not only the bath. You can pay for grooming services or do them yourself. If you'd like to try it, the following basic tips will get you started.

DOG GROOMING ESSENTIALS:

- **Dog brush:** Brushes fall into 4 main categories: regular brushes, combs, rakes, and deshedding tools. The type you use will depend on your dog's breed and coat. Get advice from your dog's breeder or a pet store clerk.
- **A good comb:** Helps to remove tangles. You may also want a flea comb to check for fleas and ticks.
- **Coat spray:** Reduces static while brushing and helps grooming tools glide more easily through fur. Many sprays also condition the coat and leave a pleasant scent.
- **Dog shampoo** and conditioner, and bath wipes for a quick clean-up.
- **Drying Supplies:** A dog blow dryer and microfiber towels.
- **Ear cleaning solution.**
- **Dog toothbrush** and toothpaste.

- **Dog nail clippers** or nail grinder, and styptic powder.
- **Animal grooming clippers** and/or shears to trim long hair.
- **Grooming table** with arm: not essential, but nice to have.

KEEP IT FUN: Keep grooming times enjoyable for both you and your dog. Schedule these when your dog is relaxed. Keep the sessions short (5-10 minutes) while your puppy is young, and gradually lengthen the time as it gets older. Teach your dog to be comfortable getting touched all over its body—this will be useful when you need to clip nails, clean ears, or for a vet exam. Praise your pup throughout the session and offer a yummy treat when it's over!

BRUSHING: Regular grooming with a brush or comb will help to keep your dog's fur in good condition. Brushing removes dirt, spreads the coat's natural oils, prevents tangles, and keeps the skin clean and irritant-free. Dogs with a smooth, short coat may only need brushing once a week. Use a *Bristle Brush* to remove dead fur and a *Slicker Brush* for tangles. Comb through the tail and longer furnishings. While brushing, also check for fleas and ticks. Some dogs require clipping or sculpting. Seek the assistance of a professional dog groomer if needed. Note: Don't forget to trim the fur around the hocks and feet if needed.

BATHING: Bathing your dog every 2-3 months is recommended. You can also bathe your dog weekly if needed. Use a gentle shampoo formulated for dogs. Here are 8 steps to make bath time enjoyable:

1. Before the bath, brush your dog well to remove dead hair and mats that easily tangle when wet.
2. Gather your bathing items—shampoo, cotton balls to place in ears to prevent water from getting in, and towels.
3. Place a rubber mat in your bath to prevent your dog from slipping. Fill the tub with about 3 inches of lukewarm water.
4. Thoroughly wet your dog to the skin. Be careful not to spray water directly in the ears, eyes, or nose.
5. Once wet, gently massage the shampoo working from head to tail, and always keep shampoo away from the eyes.
6. Rinse well, aiming to get out every bit of soap. You can apply a small amount of dog conditioner to help with combing afterward. Also, rinse well.
7. Don't forget to check the ears for any foul odor or debris. Use an ear cleaner made for dogs if needed.
8. Finish off by towel drying your dog or using a blow dryer. Hold the dryer at least a foot away (so you won't burn the skin) and monitor the heat level to ensure it's not too hot.

Note: Dogs with loose facial skin/wrinkles, such as sharp-pei or pugs, will need special attention. Clean the folds with a damp washcloth to prevent dirt and bacteria from causing irritation or infection. Then, thoroughly dry the areas between the folds.

LONG EARS: Dogs with long or floppy ears need their ears checked weekly to ensure they are clean and free of foul odor. Clean with a cotton ball moistened with a gentle ear cleaner. Ask a vet or groomer for guidance if needed.

NAIL CLIPPING: While your dog is still a puppy, get it used to have its feet touched—try a daily puppy foot massage. Once comfortable with this, use *nail trimmers* to cut off the tip of each nail at a slight angle, just before the point where it begins to curve. Take care to avoid *the quick*—the pink area (the blood vessel) running through the nail. In dogs with black nails, the quick is harder to see. If you accidentally cut the quick, it may bleed, in which case you can apply *styptic powder* to stop the bleeding. Don't forget to clip the dew claws (if your dog still has them). Dew claws do not come into contact with the ground and can quickly grow long and make your dog uncomfortable. Once you cut the nails, you could use an *emery board* to smooth the rough edges. YouTube has some helpful videos to guide you. **An alternate method** of trimming nails is by using a *nail grinder*—rotary tool that sands down the nail without cutting too close to the quick.

TOOTH BRUSHING: Dental disease, especially periodontal disease, is one of the most common diseases in dogs. Fortunately, dental disease can be reduced or prevented with regular tooth brushing. Use a soft-bristled toothbrush and doggie toothpaste—human toothpaste and baking soda can present dangers for our pets.

To begin, let your dog taste the flavored toothpaste. Then run your finger along the gums of the upper teeth. Repeat this process with a toothbrush (it takes about 30 seconds). Work from back to front, making small circles along the gum lines. Keep sessions short and offer praise and treats. Brush the teeth several times a week, or daily if possible, to help your pup get used to it. *Dental sprays* are also available to help prevent tartar build-up. Even with the best tooth brushing, your dog may need occasional professional cleaning. Your dog's dental health should be evaluated yearly by your vet.

ANAL GLANDS: Last but not least, check your dog's bottom area to make sure it is clean. Also, ensure there is no swelling since anal gland abscesses often go unnoticed in the early stages. Sometimes dogs will scoot their bottoms on the ground, indicating they may have a problem. Call your vet with any concerns. Some groomers will offer to check the anal glands and empty them.

 Download a free ebook at akc.org called "The All-Purpose Grooming Tool Kit."

16 Pet Safety Tips

1. MAKE SURE YOUR DOG HAS IDENTIFICATION. Your dog should have an identification tag with your name, address, and phone number. Also, consider permanent identification such as a Microchip. Permanent ID can be invaluable in recovering your pet in the unfortunate situation that your dog becomes lost. **Don't forget to register your dog's microchip (or tattoo) once it's implanted.**

2. KEEP YOUR DOG CONTAINED. Is your yard safe and secure? A fenced yard is a huge plus in keeping your dog safe. Walk around the border regularly to ensure there are no holes and openings for your dog to slip out. If you don't have a fence, you'll want to consider other options, such as a dog run or an invisible fence. Remember that invisible fences may keep your dog in, but do not keep intruders out. Always watch your pet regardless of your type of fence. For properties without a fence (i.e., city dwellers), stress to all family members to leash the dog when taken outdoors.

3. DOG PROOF DAILY. As mentioned on page 60, puppy-proofing your house is vital before bringing a puppy home. But puppy-proofing doesn't end there. Dogs are like forever toddlers, always getting into things. Each day you'll need to keep your eyes and ears open for potential threats to your pet (see page 87). Are the dog toys still intact? Have you scanned your yard for loose debris after parties for candy, fireworks, etc.? Is the toilet bowl shut? Being observant is a necessary part of dog ownership. Get the whole family involved in watching over your pet throughout its life.

4. TOY SAFETY. Assume your puppy will rip apart his toys and swallow any pieces it can. With that in mind, choose sturdy and safe toys—avoid toys such as those with stuffing, glass or plastic eyes, small, metal parts (i.e., springs or batteries), long strips or fibers, and chewies made of large pieces or knots of rawhide. For a full list of "OK" and "NOT OK" toys, visit akc.org/expert-advice, and search "How to Choose Safe Toys for Your Puppy."

Note: Check toys often for wear or loose parts Discard damaged toys and replace them with new ones.

5. PICK UP YOUR DOG'S WASTE. Infectious dog diseases and parasites can be transmitted via fecal matter. Keep your dog and others safe by picking up and properly disposing of your dog's waste. Don't forget your "dog poop bags" when walking your dog.

6. RESPECT LEASH LAWS. Leash laws are created to protect the public, your dog, and other dogs. Be aware of leash laws and keep your dog restrained in those areas where it is required.

7. PROVIDE GOOD SHELTER. Ideally, a dog will sleep in the home of its owner. If, however, your dog spends a lot of time outside, ensure that it has plenty of shade in the summer, warmth in the winter, and appropriate shelter.

8. NEVER LEAVE A PET IN THE CAR ON WARM DAYS. Remember, a dog is wearing a fur coat and can quickly succumb to heat stress. Even days that average 70° can be too hot for a dog, even with the car window cracked. Also, avoid walking your dog midday during a heat wave. Instead, choose a cooler time of day. *Signs of heatstroke include* excessive panting and drooling, anxiety, weakness, and abnormal gum color (darker red or even purple). Heat stroke might result in collapse and even death. All dogs outside need access to shade and plenty of cool, fresh drinking water.

9. TRAVEL SAFE. During travel, dogs should be either in a sturdy crate or attached in a car seat designed for dogs with a seat belt and harness. Never let your dog hang its head out a car window or ride in the back of a pick-up truck.

10. PREPARE FOR A DISASTER. Fire, flood, hurricanes, earthquakes, sudden illness, or injury can happen anytime. Be prepared. Keep an emergency kit handy. The kit should include a copy of your dog's health/vaccine records, clean water, enough food for a few days, a food and water bowl, an extra collar and leash, first aid items, and other essentials. The "Pet Disaster Evacuation Checklist" on page 94 can help you ready your kit.

11. KNOW BASIC FIRST AID FOR DOGS. What would you do if your pet gets a cut or wound, a burn, or ingests a harmful chemical? What if it has a seizure, is found choking, or goes into shock? Or what if you find a tick on your dog? Having some basic first aid knowledge and being equipped with the right tools can be invaluable in reducing the severity of an injury. It can also buy time until you can get to a vet. Have a pet first aid kit handy. You can purchase a pre-made kit or build your own. Call and/or visit your veterinarian when needed. See page 93 for a list of first aid pet items.

12. FIND A PET SITTER. Make sure you have someone to care for your dog if you need to go away. Give the sitter all your dog's vital information (i.e., this book, rabies certificate, vet number) in case your dog gets sick or lost. Also, have the number of a good boarding kennel or doggie daycare if needed. Pet sitter instruction printable forms are on pages 90-91.

13. KEEP AN EMERGENCY CONTACT LIST. On page 8 of this book, there is space to record your emergency contacts. This list should include people who have agreed to care for your dog in case of sudden illness, hospitalization, or other emergency. **Tip:** Print out the list and keep in a safe and visible place.

14. STAY ALERT FOR STRANGE DOGS. Sometimes, for whatever reason, a strange dog may become aggressive or even attack another dog. Stay alert, especially if you encounter an unleashed dog when on a walk. The following article offers useful advice to help you protect your dog—pethelpful.com/dogs/protecting-your-dog.

15. TEACH KIDS SAFETY AROUND DOGS. A dog is not a toy. Help children learn to be gentle with their dog (i.e., never pull a tail, ears, or rough house.) Teach kids to approach a pet nicely and not invade their space, especially when eating. Some dogs become defensive of their food and toys. As a general rule, children should never be left unsupervised with a dog. To learn more, download the online PDF of *"AKC's Safety Around Dogs Program for Kids of All Ages"* at www.akc.org.

16. HAVE A CURRENT PHOTO. Keep a good, clear, current photo of your dog readily available in case your dog gets lost. If you have a smartphone, save the picture to your phone. Know what to do if you lose your dog—See page 95.

Recognizing Signs of Sickness

NO ONE LIKES TO THINK about their dog becoming sick, but being able to recognize signs of illness can help save your pet's life. Below is a list of common healthy signs and possible causes for concern. Never hesitate to consult a vet about your dog's health.

COMMON HEALTHY SIGNS

- Alert happy attitude, excited about his favorite things
- Shiny coat without bare areas, and supple skin
- Clear, clean eyes
- Bright pink gums
- Clear breathing (i.e., no crackly coughing sounds)
- Moving freely
- Eating well, good appetite
- Regular, firm-looking stool
- Moderate weight
- Normal body temperature, between 99.5 and 102.5 ° F

POSSIBLE CAUSES FOR CONCERN

GENERAL

- Changes in energy levels, i.e. sleeping more than usual, lethargic, restless, pacing, loss of interest in favorite activities
- Weakness in limbs, i.e., limping, tripping, loss of balance
- Changes in eating, i.e., refusing to eat meals or eating less, or a sudden increase in appetite
- Weight loss

EYES AND EARS

- Cloudiness in eyes, constant tearing or yellow discharge
- Squinting, holding eye shut, swelling of eyelid

- Your dog seems unable to see where he is going
- Shaking head and scratching ears a lot
- Ears have a strong smell or drainage
- Your dog seem unable to hear well

DIGESTIVE AND URINARY

- Repeated vomiting or diarrhea
- Lack of bowel movement for 48 hours
- Worms can be seen in stool
- Increase in thirst and urination, blood in urine
- Suddenly urinating indoors or urinating more frequently

RESPIRATION/MOUTH

- Irregular breathing, i.e., panting, coughing, wheezing, sneezing
- Mouth: Foul odor, pawing at mouth, broken or loose teeth

SKIN

- Severe itching, skin that is inflamed or oozing
- Area with hair loss, bare spots, lumps or soars

IMPORTANT

- If you think your dog may have a contagious disease, call your vet ASAP. Note: You may be asked to enter their facility from a special entrance to protect others from contamination.
- Keep your vet's phone number and the after-hours emergency vet number handy. Also, plug in the address of your vet(s) into your car GPS to locate them more easily.
- If your dog shows signs of illness, contact your vet immediately.
- Record your dog's surgery or hospital stays on page 24 and veterinary exams on pages 28-57.

 A dog's normal temperature ranges from 99.5-102.5 °f.

Parasite Control Tips

PARASITES OF DOGS can cause multiple health problems, including heartworm disease, skin allergies, gastrointestinal disease, and tick-borne diseases. Some parasites can also infect family members, so it's essential to take preventative measures to protect everyone. Several factors come into play when choosing how often/when/if to administer a product. Discuss with your vet the best protocol.

ANNUAL FECAL TEST: Take your pet to the vet at least annually to be tested for parasites. If you have a concern beforehand, you can contact your vet and take a sample of your dog's feces to be tested. Record fecal tests and results on page 19.

HEARTWORM PREVENTION: Heartworm is a mosquito-borne illness that causes lung and heart disease in dogs. Prevention is fairly simple and relatively inexpensive with a monthly pill or chewable, which can protect from some or all of the most common intestinal parasites. Note: Do not begin heartworm preventatives unless your dog has already consistently been on the monthly prevention or until a heartworm test is negative. The American Heartworm Society recommends an annual heartworm blood test to screen for heartworm disease. Record screening and prevention on page 20.

INTESTINAL PARASITE CONTROL: Intestinal parasites, including roundworms, hookworms, and whipworms, are passed to dogs via infected feces. Humans are also susceptible to certain parasites. Ask your vet for guidance in choosing your dog's medication and dosage. Record deworming meds on page 18.

FLEA AND TICK PREVENTION: Based on where you live, your vet will recommend a preventative and advise which months to administer it. "Natural" flea and tick products are also available. However, make sure to discuss potential treatments with your vet beforehand. Many contain essential oils, which can irritate your dog's skin and are potentially toxic to people. Pets with true flea allergies may require a prescription flea control.

Serious illnesses such as Lyme disease are all common tick-borne diseases shared by dogs and humans. Talk to your vet about prevention and learn the proper way to remove a tick. In addition, keep a tick remover on hand and in your dog's first aid kit. Consult a vet for guidance in tick removal if needed. Record flea and tick treatments on page 21.

HOW TO REMOVE A TICK (FROM THE CDC.GOV)

1. Use fine-tipped tweezers to grasp the tick as close to the skin's surface as possible.
2. Pull upward with steady, even pressure. Don't twist or jerk the tick; this action can cause the mouth parts to break off and remain in the skin. If this happens, remove the mouth parts with tweezers. If you are unable to remove the mouth easily with clean tweezers, leave it alone and let the skin heal.
3. After removing the tick, thoroughly clean the bite area and your hands with rubbing alcohol or soap and water.
4. Never crush a tick with your fingers. Dispose of a live tick by putting it in alcohol, placing it in a sealed bag/container, wrapping it tightly in tape, or flushing it down the toilet.

PARASITE CONTROL TIPS TO PROTECT YOUR FAMILY

- **Pick up your dog's feces:** Children love to run through the yard barefoot and put things in their mouths. Be sure pet feces is picked up at least daily.
- **Cover sandboxes** and play areas to prevent animals from soiling and contaminating these areas.
- **Supervise infants** when sitting on the ground—do not let them put dirt in their mouth or eat food that has fallen.
- **Wash hands well** after exposure to soil, sandboxes, or raw meat, or after petting other dogs/animals (i.e., playing with the neighbor dog, visiting the animal shelter, or a petting zoo).

 Always pick up after your dog.

♡ Pet Insurance Guide

PET INSURANCE is one way you can find financial help with your pet's medical care. Pet insurance is different from human medical insurance however. It reimburses owners for services after they are rendered by the vet. So you'll pay the vet at the time of service and then file your claim with your insurance company. The following are some questions to consider when choosing a pet insurance.

ABOUT THE COMPANY

- How long has the company been in operation?
- Can you utilize any veterinarian and hospital?
- Do they offer multiple dog/cat discounts?
- What are the reviews from other current or former clients?

ABOUT THE POLICIES

- What are the coverage plan options?
- Can preexisting conditions be covered?
- Is preapproval of medical services ever required?
- Does the plan pay claims due to a restricted benefit schedule to actual billing?
- What are the policy limits? Is there an annual or lifetime cap for a particular medical problem?
- What are the deductible options? Does the company give you a choice of deductibles, maximums and copays?
- Will the premium increase with age or with new illnesses?
- Does the company have a well care/preventative care coverage?

ABOUT THE CLAIMS

- What is the process for filing claims and how long until the company reimburses it?
- How are claim disputes handled?
- Is there a maximum amount or reimbursement per disease/per calendar year/per incident?

WHAT'S INCLUDED AND WHAT'S NOT

- What are the breed-specific diseases excluded from coverage?
- Does the plan cover genetic conditions or chronic conditions?
- Are services associated with breeding, pregnancy, cesarean section and newborn care covered (if applicable to your needs)?
- Are costs associated with treating behavioral issues covered?
- Are consultations with specialist or emergency care covered?

Questions, source: Connecticut Valley Veterinary Associates

PET INSURANCE COMPANIES

This list is a sample of companies found online by searching "top pet insurance companies." The list is updated yearly.

- Spot - spotpetins.com
- Many Pets - manypets.com/us/
- Embrace - embracepetinsurance.com
- Pumpkin - pumpkin.care
- Healthy Paws – HealthyPawsPetInsurance.com
- Figo – FigoPetInsurance.com
- Trupanion – Trupanion.com
- Pets Best – PetsBest.com
- AKC – AKCPetInsurance.com
- Nationwide – PetInsurance.com
- Veterinary Pet Insurance (VPI) – petinsurance.com

If pet insurance is not for you, you might consider setting up a savings plan with automatic deposit or getting "Care Credit." This way you'll be prepared in case your pet needs extra care.

Notes or questions you want to ask a pet insurance company:

_____
_____
_____

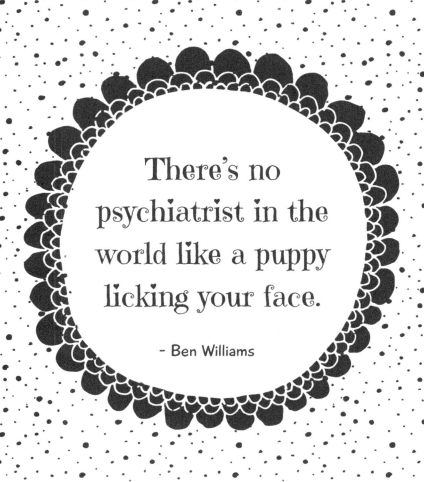

There's no psychiatrist in the world like a puppy licking your face.

- Ben Williams

PART 5
Resources and Printable Forms

NEW PUPPY CHECKLIST

PUPPY-PROOFING CHECKLIST

PET TRAVEL CHECKLIST & TO DO'S

PRINTABLE PET SITTER FORM

PRINTABLE DOG GROOMING LOG

FIRST AID KIT FOR PETS

PET DISASTER EVACUATION CHECKLIST

5 THINGS TO DO IF YOU'VE LOST/FOUND A DOG

MUST-HAVE PHONE NUMBERS & WEBSITES

NOTE SPACE FOR PET TO-DO'S

A PROMISE TO MY PET

New Puppy Checklist

YOU CAN PRINT THIS PAGE AND TAKE IT WITH YOU PET SHOPPING.

Congratulations on your new puppy! If you don't already have these items, you'll want to add them to your shopping list to help keep your precious pup happy, healthy, and safe.

- **Dog Collar and ID tag** with your information. Choose a soft adjustable collar for a young puppy. Then, a larger one as it grows older.

- **Leash:** Choose a leash with a loop that is easy to grip. At least one 4-6-foot leash and an additional longer lead for training.

- **Identification tag** with your name and address, and. A Microchip is also recommended.

- **Food and Water Bowls:** Stainless steel is a good choice. Wash daily.

- **Housetraining items:** pee pads and odor-eliminating products.

- **Containment:** Crate, puppy pen, dog gate(s).

- **Dog Toys:** Age-specific toys and chew toys—strong, durable, well-made, sized appropriately. Remove damaged toys immediately.

- **Dog Food** appropriate for your dog's developmental stage.

- **Training Treats.** Choose tiny, bite-sized treats.

- **Bedding and Snuggle Blanket:** At least 2 sets. Wash regularly.

- **Cleaning Supplies:** Use "enzymatic cleaners" to help remove urine and feces odors in case your dog has a potty accident indoors.

- **Dog Grooming Items:** You may need some or all of these items below, depending on your breed of dog. (Grooming Basics, p. 72)

    - Dog shampoo and conditioner
    - Pet grooming blow dryer
    - Towels (i.e. microfiber towels)
    - Conditioning coat spray
    - Soft-bristle brush and metal comb
    - Ear cleaning solution
    - Dog toothbrush and toothpaste
    - Dog nail grinder or nail clippers

Puppy-Proofing Checklist

Puppies, like toddlers, need constant supervision. Before you bring your puppy home, walk around each room and yard and imagine what a puppy might chew, eat, climb or pull down. Then, move those things out of reach. The following list will give you ideas what to look out for. For more information, visit akc.org/expert-advice. Search, "Household Hazards for Dogs."

- **Ensure trash cans** and recycling bins have secure locking lids. These may contain food hazards for curious puppies, such as raisins, grapes, onions, garlic, and chocolate.

- **Invest in electrical outlet covers** and secure wires and light strands. Puppies may lick an outlet or chew wires and get seriously hurt.

- **Secure furniture and decor** your puppy might pull down or knock over. Also, move open storage containers (i.e., toy bins) out of reach.

- **Make sure curtains and cords** are tied up and pulled to the side to prevent your pup from chewing or accidentally getting strangled.

- **Verify that your indoor/outdoor plants** are safe for pets. Some can be toxic for pets. Keep indoor plant pots out of reach.

- **Keep medications (human and pet)** and toiletries out of reach.

- **Secure cleaning supplies and get cabinet locks** if needed. Cleaning products can be deadly if swallowed, including 'natural" cleaners.

- **Keep cat items out of reach,** such as food, bowls, and the litter box. Cat droppings can transmit parasites and make your dog ill.

- **Check your garage.** Most products in the garage are toxic to dogs (and cats). Antifreeze and herbicides, for example, can be fatal. So lock up all products and clean any spills thoroughly. Also, secure heavy tools and store smaller items (i.e., screws, nails) high off the ground. Most importantly, always check before operating any machine. Some pups love getting underneath.

- **Be fence aware.** Look for weak spots in your fence and ensure your pool is secured to prevent drowning.

Pet Poison Helpline at 855-764-7651

Pet Travel Checklist

Before traveling or moving to a new home, verify your dog is healthy for travel and ask your vet about any health risks at your destination (i.e., heartworm). Call ahead to ensure your lodging is "pet friendly," familiarize yourself with hotel rules/fees and always clean up after your pet. For air travel, call your airline for their requirements.

- ☐ **This record book** with your pet's essential data filled in
- ☐ **Identification.** I.e., ID tags, license, tattoo, and microchip numbers
- ☐ **Collar and Leash.** Bring a spare set in case one breaks
- ☐ **Health Certificate** for travel. If required, this is obtained from your vet
- ☐ **Proof of Vaccination.** Copy of shot records and rabies certificate
- ☐ **Feeding Supplies.** Food, bottled water, treats, manual can opener, food and water bowls
- ☐ **Medications and Supplements** including preventatives, flea/tick repellant if needed, and copies of your pet's prescriptions for refills
- ☐ **Emergency numbers.** Print out a list of veterinary offices and emergency clinics where you travel. Have your vet's phone # handy
- ☐ **Poop Bags**/pooper scooper/litter box and scoop/piddle pads
- ☐ **Containment.** Crate/carrier/harness/seat belt clip for travel. Some hotels require you to crate your pet when you are out of the room
- ☐ **Grooming Tools.** I.e., brush/comb, nail clippers, toothbrush
- ☐ **Comfort Items.** I.e., favorite blanket, bedding, toys, chew items
- ☐ **Extra Sheets and Towels** to cover furniture and bedding where you are staying to protect from your dog
- ☐ **Cleaning Supplies.** I.e., paper towels, disinfectant wipes, lint roller
- ☐ **Pet Insurance** information and claims forms
- ☐ **Recent Photo** of your dog
- ☐ **Pet First Aid Kit** (see page 93) and Pet First Aid Manual

 Pet travel support: PetTravel.com, Pet Travel Hotline 1-800-545-USDA

Pet Travel To-Do List

Photocopy this page to reuse. Happy travels!

TRIP/DATE _____

Hotel Rules/Fees _____

Things to-do/Pet things to bring:

- [ ] _____
- [ ] _____
- [ ] _____
- [ ] _____
- [ ] _____
- [ ] _____
- [ ] _____
- [ ] _____
- [ ] _____
- [ ] _____
- [ ] _____
- [ ] _____
- [ ] _____
- [ ] _____
- [ ] _____
- [ ] _____

The journey of life is sweeter when traveled with a dog.

— Unknown

Pet Sitter Instruction Form

PHOTOCOPY THIS FORM TO REUSE FOR EACH PET SITTER VISIT.

MY DOG'S FEEDING SCHEDULE/ROUTINE   DATE: _____

Morning _____

_____

Midday _____

_____

Evening _____

_____

SPECIAL INSTRUCTIONS FOR PET SITTER

_____

_____

_____

_____

MY TRAVEL INFORMATION

Hotel/Location _____

Contact Number _____

Leaving/Returning on _____

Emergency Contact Pet Sitter #2 _____

Primary Vet_____Emergency Vet_____

PET SITTING MEDICAL RELEASE FORM

I,_____(pet owner) hereby give_____ (pet sitter's name) my permission to take my pet(s) to the above mentioned veterinarian (or to the closest open facility if my primary vet is not available). I give permission to the veterinarian to administer any care or medications necessary. I will assume full responsibility for the payment of veterinary services provided.

Date_____Signed_____

Pet Sitter Notes-7 Day Chart

PHOTOCOPY THIS PAGE TO REUSE FOR EACH PET SITTER VISIT.

To my sitter, please record the day and time of your visits and any concerns.

DATE	AM	NOON	MIDDAY	PM	OBSERVATIONS CONCERNS

Notes

BEST NUMBER TO REACH ME _____

Dog Grooming Log

Photocopy this page to use to track your dog's grooming.

DATE	GROOMER/PHONE	SERVICES DONE	COST

First Aid Kit for Pets

BE PREPARED for the most common pet injuries. You can purchase a pre-made first-aid kit or put one together using the guide below. Check with your vet about any medications you add to the kit. Including a **Pet First Aid Manual** is also wise. You can purchase one or download a free ebook by searching online, "AKC Pet First Aid Owners Manual." There is a *Red Cross Pet First Aid app* also available on most phone app stores.

- ☐ Water-proof storage container for kit
- ☐ Bottled water
- ☐ A rectal thermometer
- ☐ Triple antibiotic cream such as Neosporin
- ☐ Anti-bacterial cleansing wipes/Alcohol prep pads
- ☐ Peroxide
- ☐ Eye wash (e.g., saline solution)
- ☐ Self-stick Ace bandage or Vet-wrap
- ☐ Roll of gauze and sterile gauze squares (3 x 3)
- ☐ Blunt bandage scissor (to cut gauze and clip hair around wounds)
- ☐ Electric clippers (to trim fur around wounds)
- ☐ Roll of cotton
- ☐ Medical tape (1" and ½")
- ☐ Latex surgical gloves
- ☐ Emergency blanket and towel (to warm, restrain, or use as a stretcher)
- ☐ Small flashlight
- ☐ Leash and collar, soft muzzle
- ☐ Forceps (or long-handled, blunt-end tweezers) and tick remover
- ☐ Small cold pack and hot pack (self-activating)
- ☐ Copy of dog's papers & vaccination records (sealed in plastic bag)
- ☐ Card with your vet information and the poison-control number
- ☐ Medicines (ask your vet) i.e.,— Benadryl tablets for allergies, electrolyte powder (add to water on hot days)
- ☐ Clean up items, i.e., paper towels, plastic baggies

Pet Poison Helpline 855-764-7661

Pet Disaster Evacuation Checklist

Having a pre-determined plan and being prepared for an emergency or natural disaster will help you think clearly and stay calm. Tip: Keep an evacuation bag prepared and accessible in case of sudden emergency.

- ☐ Pet first aid kit (page 93) and this book
- ☐ Dog medicines(s), i.e., heartworm prevention, etc.
- ☐ Bottled water
- ☐ Feeding supplies–Dog food (1-week minimum, 2-week suggested), dog treats, food and water bowls, manual can opener
- ☐ Leashes: walking leash, short leash
- ☐ Harness (to attach to seat belt)
- ☐ Extra dog tag, (masking tape, laundry pen)
- ☐ Dog bed, blanket, and some toys
- ☐ List of dog-friendly hotels and their phone numbers, boarding facility
- ☐ Grooming items, shampoo (including waterless shampoo in case water is not readily available), brushes, etc.
- ☐ Litter and portable litter pan, poop bags
- ☐ Dog crate for travel
- ☐ Current dog photograph(s) with your contact information: useful for fliers should your dog go missing or be left at a shelter.
- ☐ Pet records stored in a waterproof container or sealable plastic bag
- ☐ Helpful Supplies–i.e., paper towels, rug cleaner, toilettes, towels, flashlight, duct tape

Visit avma.org to learn more about pets and disaster preparedness.

Emergency Disaster Hotline (800) 227-4645

5 Things To Do if You've Lost a Dog

1. Immediately put out food, water, and your dog's bed or an article of your choice at the location where your dog was last seen. There's a good chance that your dog may return.
2. Get the word out by using flyers and signs (like yard sales signs) with a picture of your dog and your phone number, and then check your phone often! Go door-to-door with flyers in the neighborhood where your dog was last seen.
3. Contact your local animal shelter, animal control facilities, vet clinics, and police departments to report missing your dog. Fax or e-mail them a photo of your dog and your contact information.
4. Instruct everyone helping you NOT to call or chase your dog. This will prolong your search. If they see your dog, tell them to sit or lay down (no eye contact) and gently toss out tasty treats to lure your dog in.
5. Post your dog on your local craigslist, in your local paper, and on other lost and found internet/Facebook sites.

5 Things To Do if You've Found a Dog

1. Check for a license or ID tag. No tags? Ask around your neighborhood in case the dog lives nearby.
2. Take the dog to the nearest veterinarian or shelter to have the dog scanned for a microchip and checked for a tattoo.
3. Notify all the proper authorities to report the dog found. Call your local police (non-emergency line). Also, call your local animal control agency (ACO) to complete a found dog report or bring the dog to them if you cannot keep the dog while researching for his/her owner.
4. Create "found dog" flyers and post them around the neighborhood and at animal service businesses.
5. Post on your local craigslist, in your local paper (found ads are often free), and on other lost and found Internet/Facebook sites.

Five Things to Do If You Have Lost or Found a Dog © Lost Dogs of America. Lostdogsofamerica.org is a free service with articles & resources on finding a lost dog.

Tip: Lost dog templates can be found online. Carva.com, for example, has free, printable lost dog flyers you can customize. Of course, prevention is the best action plan. Keep your dog under your watchful eye.

Phone Numbers Every Dog Owner Needs

EVERY DOG OWNER should keep these numbers on hand. Program them into your cell phone, include them in your dog's first aid kit, and keep a copy in your purse/wallet and the glove box of your car. Having these numbers at your fingertips could save your dog's life.

MEDICAL EMERGENCY SUPPORT

- National Animal Poison Control Center (888) 426-4435. This is a 24 hour emergency hotline. There may be a fee.
- Pet Poison Helpline (855) 764-7661. (PetPoisonHelpline.com).
- Emergency Disaster Hotline (800) 227-4645. They connect you with information and resources for pet owners affected by disasters: i.e., earthquakes, hurricanes, flooding, fire, and more.

LOST DOG SUPPORT

- National Pet Recovery Hotline (800) 984-8638. 24-hour service to help you locate your lost pet.
- Pet Amber Alert (877) 875-7387.
- AKC Companion Animal Recovery (800) 252-7894. Resources for lost dogs that are part of their registry.
- Microchip. Contact your dog's microchip company if it gets lost or to make changes to your contact information. For help finding the registry where your pet's microchip may be listed, visit the AAHA Microchip Registry Lookup at aaha.org/petmicrochiplookup.
- Stolen Pet Hotline 1-800-STOLEN-PET.
- Petfinder (800) 666-5678. (Petfinder.com). 24-hour lost and found service for members. Paid and free assistance.

PET LOSS SUPPORT

- Pet Loss Support Hotline (888) 478-7574. 24-hour hotline. Emotional support for those who've lost a pet.

DOG TRAINING SUPPORT

- Dog Training Hotline (212) 727-7257. (TheDogSite.com). Free dog owners training, resources, and referral helpline provided by the American Dog Trainers Network.
- Animal Behavior Hotline (312) 644-8338. Free service to pet owners experiencing behavior issues with their dogs or cats.

PET TRAVEL SUPPORT

- Pet Travel Hotline 1-800-545-USDA. Before traveling by plane with your dog, call with questions about transporting your pet, what papers you need to provide, what to bring, etc.
- Pet Airways (888) 738-2479. (PetAirways.com). Pet-only airline.
- Pet Travel Information (877) 241-0184. (PetTravel.com). Worldwide resource for traveling with pets.

OTHER IMPORTANT NUMBERS

- Spay/Neuter Helpline 1-800-248-SPAY: National referral service for free or low-cost spay and neuter services.
- Animal Legal Hotline (707) 795-2533: Call if you think someone is mistreating a dog or other animal or want to report a pet professional you think is acting illegally or unethically.

YOUR VET'S INFORMATION AT A GLANCE

MY VET'S NAME/PHONE _____

EMAIL _____

ADDRESS _____

_____

EMERGENCY VET PHONE _____

ADDRESS _____

_____

Tip: Program the address of the ER Vet Clinic into your car GPS so you can get there easily.

TIP: PRINT OUT THIS PAGE WITH THE PHONE NUMBERS AND KEEP HANDY.

Websites Every Dog Owner Needs

These are only a sample of the numerous online websites available to pet owners. Have fun learning and pet shopping!

HEALTH
- VetStreet.com - Pet owner health and wellness resources
- PetMD.com - Pet health and wellness articles
- AAHA.org - Canine Vaccination Guidelines
- Healthypet.com - Vet articles from the experts at AAHA
- AVMA.org - American Veterinary Medical Association
- AHVMA.org - American Holistic Veterinary Medical Association
- Petsandparasites.org – Information/resources on parasites
- PetPoisonHelpline.com (855) 764-7661

TRAINING
- AVSAB.org - American Veterinary Society of Animal Behavior
- AKC.org - American Kennel Club. Dog Owners Resource Center
- TheDogSite.com - The American Dog Trainers Network
- Apdt.com - The Association of Professional Dog Trainers

LOST DOG SUPPORT
- PetAmberAlert.com
- Missinganimalresponse.com
- Lostdogsofamerica.com
- Helpinglostpets.com
- Lostcatfinder.com (In case you have a kitty)

PET ADOPTION/RESCUE
- AdoptaPet.com - Connects homeless pets with caring owners
- PetFinder.com - Connects you with waiting to be adopted pets
- AKC.org/akc-rescue-network/

MICROCHIP COMPANIES
- AKC Reunite - AKCReunite.org
- Avid - Avidid.com
- Home Again - HomeAgain.com
- AAHA Microchip Registry Lookup - aaha.org/petmicrochiplookup

FAVORITE PET SHOPPING SITES

- Chewy.com
- OnlyNaturalPet.com
- Amazon.com
- EntirelyPets.com
- IHeartDogs.com
- 1800PetMeds.com (Online pet pharmacy)
- WalmartPetRx.com (to order pet meds online)
- PetCare.RX Online Animal Pharmacy

GENERAL DOG CARE/LIFESTYLE

- PetDiets.com - Info on healthy dog diets (i.e. homemade)
- DogFoodAdvisor.com – Dog food reviews and advice
- Dogsters.com - Educates on how to best care for your dog
- ModernDogMagazine.com - Diverse topics/training tips
- Rover.com - Dog sitting/dog walking/home boarding information
- BringFido.com - Resource for pet and owner travel planning
- PetTravel.com - Worldwide resource for traveling pets
- PetAirways.com - Pet only airline
- Akc.org - The American Kennel Club: registry of pedigreed purebred dogs and resources for dog owners
- DogBreedInfo.com - Educates dog owners about dog breeds

PET INSURANCE COMPANIES (see page 82 for more companies)

- Figo – FigoPetInsurance.com
- Trupanion – Trupanion.com
- Pets Best – PetsBest.com
- AKC – AKCPetInsurance.com
- Veterinary Pet Insurance (VPI) – petinsurance.com

Resources provided in this book are for informational purposes only and do not necessarily represent the views of the author or publisher.

My Pet Notes

My Pet Notes

My little dog—a heartbeat at my feet.
—Edith Wharton

My Pet Notes

My Pet Notes

A dog will teach you unconditional love. If you can have that in your life, things won't be too bad.
—Robert Wagner

My Pet Notes

_____
_____
_____
_____
_____
_____
_____
_____
_____
_____
_____
_____
_____
_____
_____
_____
_____
_____
_____
_____
_____
_____
_____
_____

Dogs embody unconditional love. Caring for them well is how we honor, cherish, and return their love.

—Leila Grandemange

A Promise to My Pet

AKC Responsible Dog Owner Pet Promise © American Kennel Club.

- I will never overlook my responsibilities for this living being and recognize that my dog's welfare is totally dependent on me.
- I will always provide fresh water and quality food for my dog.
- I will socialize my dog via exposure to new people, places, and other healthy dogs.
- I will take pride in my dog's appearance with regular grooming.
- I will recognize the necessity of basic training by teaching my dog to reliably sit, stay and come when called.
- I will take my dog to the vet regularly and keep all vaccinations current.
- I will pick-up and properly dispose of my dog's waste.
- I will make sure my dog is regarded as an AKC Canine Good Citizen by being aware of my responsibilities to my neighbors and to the community.
- I will ensure that the proper amount of exercise and mental stimulation appropriate for my dog's age, breed and energy level is provided.
- I will ensure that my dog has some form of identification (which may include collar, tags, tattoo, or microchip ID.)
- I will adhere to local leash laws.

About the Author

Leila Grandemange is an award-winning dog writer, a member of the Dog Writers Association of America (DWAA), and a recipient of the *AKC Responsible Dog Ownership Public Service Award*.

From an early age, Leila's life has been intertwined with the world of animals. Whether riding and tending to horses, caring for her beloved dogs, or participating in canine sports and pet therapy, she has developed a profound appreciation for the immense joy and responsibility of sharing life with these loyal companions. Through her heartfelt writing and love for animals, Leila shares invaluable guidance to pet lovers and uplifting dog lover faith stories! **Discover more about Leila's books by exploring her works on Amazon and visiting her website at LeilaGrandemange.com.**

Do you have more than one dog? Add the BLUE COVER edition of this book to distinguish your pets records, ISBN: 978-0-9975658-3-6.

Acknowledgments

Tail wagging thanks to Dr. Jamie Adkins, DVM, Dr. Virginia Nunez, DVM, and Dr. David Hernke, DVM for sharing their veterinary expertise.

IMAGE CREDITS: Cover image © gollykim. Girl playing with dog © Jacklooser. Sick dog © Togatelu. Cartoon Dogs © MarinaDreams. Dog loving boy © Jacklooser. Boy picking up waste © Victor Brave. Family ©Kateryna Davydenko. Frames and stardust, Lisa Glanz. ER Cross and Heart Doodles by Freepik.

Puppies

are a gift from above, entrusted to us like precious seeds. We water them with praise, patience, and love, and watch them grow into full bloom.

—Leila Grandemange

Made in the USA
Las Vegas, NV
17 February 2024